To Maree, my mother,
for showing us how funny and enchanting life can be.

Winkle's World

Lara Jo Regan

By Mr. Winkle,
as told to Michael Regan

RANDOM HOUSE  NEW YORK

Walk
with me
through
Winkle's
World

Bright-eyed and bushy-tailed—that's how I try to emerge every morning from my pup tent. I've got "bushy-tailed" down pat. The "bright-eyed" part usually takes a few minutes to kick in.

Dear Mr. Winkle. You ARF the cutest dog alive! My birthday is p Can you come to m

Some mailmen avoid houses with dogs. But not our e-mailman. Every day he stuffs my in-box with hundreds of messages from all over the world. It makes my heart wag when people take the time to write. So I do my best to answer each and every message. When my paws get too tired, I type with my tongue.

I enjoy a good meal as much as the next chowhound. But my tongue has lousy aim, so my mom hand-feeds me, morsel by morsel, to reduce cleanup time. I offer to return the favor with my paws when it's time for her to eat, but she always sticks with a fork and spoon.

Most people think dogs exploit trees and fire hydrants. Truth is, we share a complex spiritual relationship with them. Here I am conducting my morning sniff ritual with my favorite palm tree, asking permission to adjust its aura.

I guess everyone's life needs a little drama. The conflict in Winkle's World

comes courtesy of my stepbrother, Clark Cat. Here he is, throwing a hissy fit

during a family portrait. I try to be nice to Clark Cat, but he usually just responds

with meows and pussycat pranks. Yesterday, he called my pup tent a mutt hut!

I'm getting ready to go see my grandma. So I better get a

short-back-and-sides for my monthly grooming. Last time

I visited, she said I looked like a hippie hamster.

Walks rule, no matter what the weather. Especially when they lead to Grandma's house.
I just hope this raincoat doesn't muss up my new fur-do or attract any big bad wolves.

GRANDMA! What a Big Tooth You Have!

I may be an orphan, but I've got a huge foster family of wonderful creatures

from all over the world. Meet my adoptive grandma, Precious. She's over

twenty years old and has only one tooth left. (She had to retire from her job

as a watchdog.) I love my grandma!

Most folks think I'm just a puppy. But my friend Pickles the Pig knows that I'm a full-grown adult. She even asked me to serve as "best man" at her wedding. None of the rental places in town stocked a size ⅛ tuxedo, so Mom made me one at home that fit nice and snug. Unfortunately, the back door of the limo fit Pickles a little *too* snugly. I just practiced my wedding toast while they tried to get her unstuck.

We finally made it to the church, but that swine of a groom never showed! I tried to cheer up Pickles with a "there's plenty of other pigs in the sty" pep talk. But all she did was chomp on her bridal bouquet and trample the wedding cake. Poor Pickles!

Time to Paws...

That no-show groom bummed me out so badly I had to go to my favorite thinking spot. I decided to send Pickles a dozen truffles in a heart-shaped box of mud. And I cheered myself up by remembering to stop and smell the roses— especially the ones whose petals have fallen to the ground.

Speaking of things that cheer me up, here's my pal Wheely Willy! He's the most happening dude I know. Willy's back legs don't work anymore, so his mom built him this cool rear axle. Now he wheels around so fast I can hardly keep up with him on our walks. "Hey, Willy, *wait for ME!*"

Clark Cat

told me baths were great. But

I think he was just trying to trick me.

I guess I tricked him, though, 'cause I'm

having a great time scrubbing up for my

photo shoot tomorrow. I even scored a

cool new mohawk! Don't tell

my grandma.

Being an international dog of mystery, I spend a lot of time on the road and in the air. So I've learned to stay calm during long layovers, rough landings, and boneless in-flight meals.

For ground transport, I cruise in my very own fur-lined, air-conditioned travel bag. It's like my mini mobile-home-away-from-home.

This sure is a nice hotel, except room

service doesn't offer kibble omelets.

I figure maybe I can snag a little of

Mom's breakfast while she's on the

phone. I'm staying away from the

coffee, though. Last time I snuck a

sip of that stuff, I chased a dust

bunny around for over an hour until

I realized that it was just my tail!

ERVICE

CaNine-to-Five

All in a dog day's work.

9:30 a.m. Bookstore appearance
"Can I have your pawtograph?"

1 p.m. Judging fifth-grade
Winkle-drawing contest
"They all look good to me!"

4 p.m. Interview with
Dogue magazine
"Who does your fur?"

HOME WOOF HOME

I love traveling and meeting my fans. But it sure is great to get back to my own pad. I can't wait to take walks, sniff my favorite trees, and play with my friends.

All *right*! It's my best buds, Murray and Fred! We get together every week to romp

and howl at delivery trucks and trade bone stories. Murray claims he dug up a

dinosaur bone last weekend. But Fred told me it was just an old Wiffle ball bat.

Clark Cat

and I finally found

something in common—we both love naps.

So now whenever he gets mad at me and I get

mad at him for being mad at me, we just sleep it off.

Once I tried counting sheep
to fall asleep, but my instincts took over and
I woke up and started herding them. So now when I need
some shut-eye, I just think about all the beautiful things
and great adventures and magical creatures I came
across that day. I always nod off long before
I can count them all.

Another day begins in Winkle's World...

The End

Published in the United States by Random House, Inc., New York, and simultaneously in Canada by Random House of Canada Limited, Toronto.
www.randomhouse.com/kids
www.mrwinkle.com
Library of Congress Control Number: 2001093771
ISBN: 0-375-81543-0 (trade) — ISBN: 0-375-91543-5 (lib. bdg.)
Printed in the United States of America First Edition May 2002 10 9 8 7 6 5 4 3 2 1
RANDOM HOUSE and colophon are registered trademarks of Random House, Inc.
Mr. Winkle and his likeness are trademarks of Lara Jo Regan.
Photos on pages 10 and 36 by Thomas Michael Alleman

Design by Mika Toyoura Mingasson